Contents

Icons Key

Throughout this *Whole Life Worship Study Guide* you will see the two icons below. The first indicates the approximate time each activity will take you and the second where there is an animated video available to watch on our website.

 Duration

 Videos on licc.org.uk/wholelifeworship

Session One:
Worshipping Engages
Our Whole Lives

Aim

To see that worship is a response to God's mercy and involves the whole of our lives.

Materials

Bibles

Pens

Post-it Notes

Core Text

Romans 12:1-2

Introduction ⏱ 20 MIN

Worship is a central theme in the Bible. It's found explicitly on many pages, and implicitly on all. It's to be found in every stage of God's big story: from Eden, where Adam and Eve live before God and one another without distance or shame; to Egypt, where the groans of slaves catch the ear of Heaven. From the wilderness, where God's Law is fearfully received; to Israel, where a nation under God is established. From Jesus, who only does what he sees his Father doing; to the ends of the earth, where disciples of this Jesus are made. And ultimately, to the glorious garden-city, where sin and death are no more, and people from every tribe and tongue dwell in the light and presence of the Lord God Almighty and the Lamb.

It's big, it's glorious, it's central. It's what we are made for! So it's pretty important that we fully understand it... and not just understand it, but live it.

- Split into twos and threes, with each mini-group looking at one of the following passages. Taking a few minutes to discuss it, summarise in one sentence what the passage says about worship, before sharing with the whole group.

Psalm 95:1-7
1 Kings 18:30-38
Amos 5:21-24

Generally speaking, we recognise we are worshipping when we sing a song in church, but not when we sign off the accounts; when we are praying for an overseas missionary, but not when we are paying for our shopping. But as the passages we looked at show, worship is wide-ranging, and can cover all aspects of who we are and what we do.

Video (optional) 📹 🕐 5 MIN

Watch Video One: Worshipping Engages Our Whole Lives
Available at: licc.org.uk/wholelifeworship

- What struck you as you watched the video?

"Biblical worship is... a response to God's revelation of himself, empowered by the Holy Spirit, which finds expression in every aspect of human life and experience."

—

John Risbridger

Bible Study 🔘 40 MIN

Read Romans 12:1-2

Some members of the group may be very familiar with this passage, and may have even studied it in a fair amount of detail. The great thing about Romans 12:1-2 is that it is like a great piece of art; every time we return to it there is something new to be seen!

Having outlined in chapters 1-11 the grand sweep of God's spectacular redemptive actions in human history, Paul starts off his appeal to a new way of life by reminding Christians that Christian worship is a response: it is 'in view' of God's outrageous wisdom and mercy.

• What are some of the highlights of what God has done for us? Feel free to flick through Romans 1-11.

• Why do you think Paul says we need to keep these things 'in view'?

Having reminded us of what God has done and that we must keep this 'in view', Paul goes on to talk about our response. He says that our lives (literally bodies) should become a sacrifice. The Christians that Paul wrote to in Rome, whether they were from a Gentile or Jewish background, would have had a particular understanding of sacrifice. Almost without exception, offering a sacrifice was a clear-cut, one-off moment. You bring your animal/produce, a priest offers it to the 'god' in question, and it is then cooked and consumed – a 'supply, die and fry' model if you like.

• Although we don't offer sacrifices in this way anymore, we might be tempted to see Sunday and our church activities as more significant to God than the rest of the week. How might this passage challenge us to think differently?

Note that the sacrifice is **offered.** Our living for God is not something that just happens automatically, it's something we must choose to give him.

• What might this mean for you in your day-to-day life?

Our sacrifice is also **holy and pleasing.** It is amazing to think that God views our lives in this way. The reason why we are able to live lives that are holy and pleasing is because of the holy and pleasing sacrifice that has already been made for us and because God's Holy Spirit lives within us (cf. Romans 3:20-26; 4:23-5:2; 5:8-11; 5:16-19; 8:1-4).

• What do you think is significant about the fact that the sacrifice is **living?**

Looking Ahead ⏱ 10 MIN

- What might it look like for you to worship God this week in your work, study, chores or relationships?

God calls us to worship him in the ordinary everyday areas of life. So it makes sense that the time that we spend together as Christians encourages and equips us for these activities and places. How might this understanding of whole life worship affect:

- Our worship together on Sundays?

- The things we talk and pray about in small groups?

Prayer ⏱ 10 MIN

On a post-it/scrap of paper, write down your name and a couple of things that you will be doing this week that you generally find easy to see as acts of worship.

On the other side, write down one or two things that you will be doing this week where you generally find it hard to feel like you are worshipping.

When everybody is done, put these notes together in the middle. Take some time to thank God for his incredible mercy. Ask that, in the light of his mercy, he will help you to respond by offering yourselves as living sacrifices.

Takeaway

Take the post-its and randomly assign them around the group, making sure you don't have your own.

During the week, pray for the person whose note you have and for the activities they will be doing. Perhaps you could send them an encouraging message at some point.

Session Two: Worshipping Offers Us Fresh Insight

Aim
To see that worship enables us to see the world differently – in the light of God's big story, and how we play our part.

Materials
Bibles

Core Text
Ephesians 1:15-23

Introduction 🕐 15 MIN

- What is your favourite story (whether book, film or TV series) and in what ways has it impacted you?

Stories have incredible power to draw us in – this is why it's very hard not to listen in when someone is telling a story in the staff kitchen or at the end of a class. Stories also have incredible power to transform us. They offer us a new perspective on life, stir our emotions, and may prompt us to act differently – we may speak slightly more eloquently after watching 'The Crown,' or decide not to go on a cruise after watching 'Titanic'!

The Bible, of course, tells a big story, a story that can radically shape the way we think, feel and live. But the Bible isn't the only story we get caught up in. Every culture has its own story/stories that attempt to explain the origin, purpose and destiny of human life, and these shape us too.

- Think about someone you know well who is not a Christian. How do they understand the origins, purpose and destiny of life? How do their beliefs shape their actions and priorities?

Sometimes, when we meet together as Christians, our times of gathered worship can simply become a form of escaping from the world and its stories. But God's intention for these times goes much deeper than that: in our worship our eyes and hearts are drawn into God's great story, and when this happens, we see life in a new light.

Video (optional) 📺 🕐 5 MIN

Watch Video Two: Worshipping Offers Us Fresh Insight
Available at: licc.org.uk/wholelifeworship

- What struck you as you watched the video?

"Worship is subject that should dominate our lives seven days a week."

—

David Peterson, *Engaging with God*

Bible Study ⓖ 45 MIN

Read Ephesians 1:15-23

Ephesians 1:15-23 is one of several prayers of Paul recorded in the New Testament. It follows an outpouring of praise, reminding the believer of God's incredible redemption story (1:3-14). In his prayer, Paul prays that we might know the author of this story (v17), see the goodness of the story (v18), and be filled with God's power so that we can play our part in the story (vs19-23). This chapter presents us with a great example of how the Bible doesn't merely inform our minds but also thrills our hearts and inspires our prayer, our worship, and our life.

Know the author of the story (v17)

- The 'gods' that were worshipped in the ancient world were often depicted as distant, impersonal and uninvolved. In what ways does v17 show that God is not like this?

- How might being reminded that God is not distant or impersonal affect our worship?

See the goodness of the story (v18)

- The stories that the Ephesian people believed did not generally inspire much hope. Look back at vs13-14. What is it about God's story that gives us hope?

- In what ways do worship services remind us of the goodness of God's story?

Be filled with power to play your part in the story (vs19-23)

We know from archaeology and ancient texts (including the book of Acts) that Ephesus was a place where people lived in fear of evil spirits. The magic and superstition practised were based on fear, manipulation and control: trying to gain leverage over spirits in order to get them to do what they wanted, namely leave them alone but harm their enemies!

- In light of this, what do you think is the significance of Paul's description of God's power and Christ's position above all things?

- How is God's power accessed, who is it available to, and what is it for?

- How might this set us free from seeing life and God through a lens of fear, manipulation and control?

Looking Ahead ⏱ 10 MIN

Theologian-philosopher James K. A. Smith says that gathered worship plays a key role in 're-storying' us: it reminds us of who we are, of who God is and what life is ultimately about. Regular reminders of God's story in gathered worship fuel and direct our desire to live for God in the world.

- Having thought about the ways that worship draws us back into the story of God, how might that affect your engagement with Sunday worship services?

- If Jesus really is above everything, how will this shape the way that you pray in church services and as a small group?

- How might this hope we've reflected on transform our everyday lives this week?

Takeaway

When you are next attending a church service, do the following:

- Before the service: Pray that you and fellow-worshippers will be shaped by God's story.

- During the service: Be on the lookout for elements of God's story being communicated through the songs, prayers, liturgy, sermon, sacraments, decorations, architecture etc. Think about how these might inspire and shape you for what you will be doing in the coming week.

- After the service: Write down one or two things you noticed. Refer back to these during the week and use them as prayer points. It would also be very encouraging for the person/people leading the service if you let them know a way that the service was helpful to you.

Prayer ⏱ 10 MIN

Use the passage as a basis for your prayers.

- Pray that you may know God, see the goodness of his story and be filled with power to play your part within it.

- Pray for your church and all involved in leading worship activities, that God will inspire and guide them.

- Pray for yourselves, that your small group gatherings and church worship services will continue to shape your thinking and living.

Session Three:
Worshipping Transforms
Our Ordinary Actions

Aim

To see how worship flows from understanding our identity as beloved children of God into 'whatever we do.'

Materials

Bibles

Core Text

Colossians 3:12-17

Feedback (optional)

If you have attended a church service since you last met as a group, did anybody notice any elements of God's story being communicated during the service?

Introduction 🕐 15 MIN

It's one thing to believe that anything we do can be a way of worshipping God. But to think, feel and live this reality in the midst of the tasks and jobs we do during the week is not always easy. We get tired, bored, distracted, frustrated and so on. This means it can be much easier to feel like we are worshipping God when we sing, pray and take communion in church services than it does when we are inputting data, packing a lunch box or walking a customer to where the ground almonds are located.

Think about a task that you perform regularly, whether it's something in your workplace, in your voluntary activities, or something around the home or garden.

- To what extent do you typically see it as a form of worship?

- What makes an action an act of worship?

Video (optional) 📹 🕐 5 MIN

Watch Video Three: Worshipping Transforms Our Ordinary Actions
Available at: licc.org.uk/wholelifeworship

- What struck you as you watched the video?

Bible Study ⏱ 45 MIN

Read Colossians 3:12-17

Though small in size, the letter to the Colossians beautifully reveals the depths of Christ's love, the scope of his mission and his absolute centrality to all of life. Jesus changes everything: bringing freedom, meaning, hope and a whole new way of living. We don't know exactly who was in the congregation to whom Paul wrote, but we do know that at least a good number were slaves.

Slavery was common in the Roman Empire. Historians estimate that between a third to over half of the population were slaves. They did a wide range of jobs, including cooking, childcare, teaching, mining, practising medicine, farming and asset management. Conditions varied greatly: some fared well under thoughtful owners, whereas others were subjected to incredibly harsh treatment, including physical beatings and sexual abuse. Regardless of what they did or how they were treated, slaves had no legal rights and were thought of as 'speaking tools' rather than people worthy of dignity and respect.

- What does Paul say about our identity as Christians in 3:12?

- Bearing in mind the people he was writing to here, what impact might his words have had upon the way they viewed themselves?

- 3:12-16 describes actions and characteristics appropriate for God's chosen, holy and dearly loved people. What are these?

- According to these verses, what role can gathered worship play in helping us to become people who live and act this way?

Take a look at verse 17

- What do you think it means to do all things 'in the name of the Lord Jesus'?

- How might this help you see your day-to-day tasks in a fresh light?

Looking Ahead ⏱ 10 MIN

- How might seeing your day-to-day tasks as worship help you to feel more connected to God throughout the week?

- What could you do to remind yourself at the start, middle and/or end of the day that we worship God through our actions?

- As a group, how could you help one another in this?

Prayer ⏱ 10 MIN

Use the verses below, each of which refer to our hands, to guide you in your prayers for the things you have been discussing and the tasks that lie ahead this week. You may find it helpful to read one verse, have one or two people pray around it, then read the next one, pray again, and so forth.

Commit to worship: 'I will praise you as long as I live, and in your name I will lift up my hands.' (Psalm 63:4)

Pray

We may sin, but through Christ we may know forgiveness: 'Who may ascend the hill of the Lord? Who may stand in his holy place? He who has clean hands and a pure heart.' (Psalm 24:3-4)

Pray

God grants us strength and courage: 'They were all trying to frighten us, thinking, "Their hands will get too weak for the work, and it will not be completed." But I prayed, "Now strengthen my hands."' (Nehemiah 6:9)

Pray

We depend on God: 'Yet you, Lord, are our Father. We are the clay, you are the potter; we are all the work of your hand.' (Isaiah 64:8)

Pray

Takeaway

One way that Christians throughout the centuries have found helpful to reflect on where God has been at work in the ordinary is the 'Prayer of Examen'. It can help us become more 'tuned in' to where God is at work in the present too.

This week, aim to set aside 5-10 minutes at some point each evening to try this. Don't worry if you miss a day; just pick it up again the next day.

There are various ways to practise the Examen but the following is a simple guide that focuses on thanksgiving. Try to keep your focus on thanksgiving. If during the Examen you suddenly remember that there are things that you need to do or things that you want to pray about, consider doing it afterwards when you have finished.

The Prayer of Examen

• Find a quiet and comfortable place to sit, put your phone on silent. If you live with other people, give them strict instructions not to interrupt you!

• Take a moment just to breathe, allowing your muscles to relax.

• Thank God that he loves you and has been with you throughout the day.

• Cast your mind back over the day, starting from the moment you woke up. Mentally re-live the highlights of your day, taking a moment to pause and think about the ways that God was with you and blessing you at various points. Allow yourself to enjoy these moments again and thank God for them.

• If something comes to mind which did not go so well, perhaps something you ought not to have said or someone you hurt, ask for God's forgiveness and be ready to receive his grace.

• Stop when you arrive back at the present.

• If you wish, you may want to jot down particular things that stood out.

Session Four: Worshipping Inspires Our Everyday Speech

Aim

To explore how gathered worship can shape the words we say and think everyday in more Christ-like ways.

Materials

Bibles

Core Text

James 5:13-18

Feedback (optional)

Did anybody have a go at doing the Examen? How did it go?

Introduction ⏱ 10 MIN

Think about one or more of the situations below. What kind of conversation would you be most likely to have with the other person?

- A family member, let's call him Sean, has a reputation for being unreliable, and one day he forgets to pick you up from the train station. Another family member comes to pick you up and on the journey home brings up the subject of Sean's reliability.

- You're having coffee with a work colleague. The boss you both share is unpredictable and has a tendency to lash out when under stress... which seems to be quite often. You're both usually on the receiving end.

- You're waiting at the school gate with a parent of a child in the same class as yours. You're concerned about what's going on in the classroom as their newly qualified teacher seems to be struggling with a small group of disruptive children in the class.

In this session, we will be looking at a short passage in James and then thinking about how this connects to our Sunday worship. James's letter talks a lot about how we respond to a whole range of circumstances: testing times, temptations, encountering people in need, power struggles within church communities, conversations that hold the potential for conflict, recognising sin in ourselves, recognising sin in others, and more besides. Pretty much every response we make involves words, whether we say them out loud or keep them quiet; whether we say them to ourselves, to others or to God. Pound for pound, James probably talks about these responses to day-to-day situations more than any other book in the Bible.

Video (optional) 🎬 ⏱ 5 MIN

Watch Video Four: Worshipping Inspires Our Everyday Speech
Available at: licc.org.uk/wholelifeworship

- What struck you as you watched the video?

"Words which do not give the light of Christ increase the darkness."

—

Mother Teresa

Bible Study 🕐 45 MIN

Read James 5:13-18

In his letter, James builds on and applies teaching found in books like Proverbs and the gospels, which reveal a close link between our hearts and the words we speak (cf. Proverbs 15:28, Luke 6:45). Genuine faith shapes the direction of actions and words. This connection between our hearts and our words is two-way: our words reveal something of what is in our hearts, and our words, for better or worse, have the power to shape our hearts (and the hearts of others).

Take a look at James 4:1-6

- What is the danger of always speaking the words that are in our heads and hearts?

- Do we find ourselves regularly complaining, or speaking words that betray a sense of anxiety or fear? What might this say about what is happening in our hearts?

Now look at James 5:13-18

Here, we are presented with a new way, God's desired way, of responding to a number of circumstances.

- In what ways do these godly responses build faith and grow community? How do they contrast with the responses you looked at in 4:1-3?

- Looking at the various responses in 5:13-15, which one do you think comes most easily? Which one do you think would feel the most unnatural?

- Why do you think it might be important to respond in these ways, even when you don't feel like it?

Looking Ahead 🕐 15 MIN

- As we have already seen, the condition of our hearts shapes the words that we say. What things get said or sung in your church services that condition your heart to respond in a more godly way to the circumstances of life?

- How might the conversations you've had in the group in this session impact your worship on Sunday?

- Is there a particular situation that you are facing where you would like to respond differently than usual?

Prayer 🕙 10 MIN

Have one or two people in the group read out the words which are not in bold. Everyone else reads the words that are in bold. After you have encouraged one another with these words, pray that by God's Word and Spirit, he will continue to condition your hearts through worship to enable you to respond and speak well in your daily lives.

Are you in trouble?
Go ahead and speak to God!
Go ahead and pray.

Are you happy?
Go ahead and speak to God!
Go ahead, sing songs of praise.

Are you ill?
Go ahead and speak to God!
Call friends over to pray for you.

Do you have faith?
Go ahead and speak to God!
He will make you well.

Have you done wrong?
Go ahead and speak to God!
He will forgive you.

Do you have brothers and sisters in Christ?
Go ahead and speak to God!
Speak to God for each other.

Are you forgiven and right with God?
Go ahead and speak to God!
Your words will be powerful and effective.

Elijah was a human being, just like you and me. He went ahead and spoke to God, asking for it not to rain. It did not rain for three and a half years! Then, he went ahead and spoke to God and it started raining again, and the plants started growing again.

So, whatever is going on in our lives, what should we do?
Go ahead and speak to God!

Takeaway

In the next church service that you attend, keep your eyes and ears open for words that will condition your heart, making you more likely to respond well to situations on your frontline. Perhaps you could talk about what you notice with someone from your group at the end of the service or when you next meet?

Session Five:
Worshipping Focuses
Our Wavering Hearts

Aim

To explore how true worship of
God is fuelled by love and how
worship also inspires a deeper
love for God and others.

Materials	Core Text
Bibles	Revelation 2:1-7

Feedback (optional)

Think back to Sunday: did you notice anything that was said, seen or sung
in the service that would be helpful in conditioning your heart, making
you more likely to respond well to situations on your frontline?

Introduction ⏱ 10 MIN

Imagine you have just moved to a new area and you have been looking
online to find local churches. You come across a church called St. Perfecto,
and they have a very impressive and up-to-date website. That Sunday you
turn up and the building is both beautiful and functional and includes some
very comfortable seating. A team of children's workers provide a fun time
for the young ones while the adults listen to a doctrinally sound sermon,
delivered by the impeccably dressed senior leader. At the end of the service,
you enjoy an unusually high quality cup of tea/coffee before you leave. The
experience seemed to tick so many boxes... except for one thing: you're left
with a vague sense that a genuine love for God and people had somehow
been lost along the way.

- If you were invited to preach at St. Perfecto what sorts of things would
  you want to say to them?

Video (optional) 📺 ⏱ 5 MIN

Watch Video Five: Worshipping Focuses Our Wavering Hearts
Available at: licc.org.uk/wholelifeworship

- What struck you as you watched the video?

"Were the whole realm of nature mine, that were an offering far too small; Love so amazing, so divine, demands my soul, my life, my all."

—

Isaac Watts

"If worship forms us to be a people who dwell in that reign, then we will carry God's kingdom wherever we go – and we will be equipped to reach out to the culture around us with words of gospel truth and deeds of gospel faithfulness. God grant our churches such worship – for his glory and for the love of the world."

—

Marva J. Dawn

Bible Study ⏱ 45 MIN

The church in Ephesus made a great start despite severe challenges from the off. We know from Acts chapters 19 and 20 that Paul spent a long time teaching there (2–3 years) and specifically warned the elders of the church about the dangers of false teachers (20:28-31). In this church's early years, we see not only a hunger for knowledge, but also a heart of love (Acts 20:36-38 and Ephesians 1:15-16). It is also widely believed that the Apostle John, who writes about love so much in his gospel and letters, was an overseer of the Ephesian church for some time. However, by the time John's letter to the church in Ephesus in Revelation 2 is read to them near the end of the first century, some things have changed.

Read Revelation 2:1-7

- In what areas has the Ephesian church excelled? What have they failed to hold on to?

- What will be their punishment if they fail to repent? Why do you think it's so severe?

- What will be their reward if they do repent? Why is this reward so special (it may help you to refer to Genesis 3:22-24 and Revelation 22:15)?

- Imagine that you were part of this church back then, how would you have felt hearing these words read to you?

We don't know exactly what was meant by losing their first love. The emphasis could be on their love for Jesus, their love for those within the church or even their love for those outside of the church. However, we know from the rest of the Bible and from our experience that love for God and others is inseparable (1 John 4:7-21).

- Why do you think Jesus was so exercised by this loss of their first love?

- How do you think it's possible that they could be doing so much good stuff but not notice such an important change had taken place?

Time and again God calls his people back to their love relationship with him.

- In what ways do you think our worship together can strengthen our love for God, focus our wavering hearts?

- Are there any ways in which you think you might be distracted by superficial things in your Sunday worship?

- In what ways does your Sunday worship guard the priority of love?

- What differences do you notice in worship when you are caught up in the joy of God's love for you?

Looking Ahead ⏱ 10 MIN

- As we encounter Christ's love in gathered worship, how does this impact our capacity to love others in our day-to-day lives? Is there anything you can do to help this process happen more?

Prayer ⏱ 15 MIN

At the end of this series, where you have been exploring how Sunday worship services connect with and shape us for everyday life, spend some time together praying about the following:

- Thank God for his interest in the whole of your lives and how you see God at work in your church and in your daily lives.

- Repent of ways in which you are failing to love God and the people he has made, whether inside or outside of church.

- Ask God to help you grow in worship together on Sundays in ways that will help you worship him more lovingly wherever you are, Monday to Saturday.

Takeaway

- Think about one thing that you want to remember from this series of studies or want to commit to doing differently. What things might help you to keep remembering/doing this?

Ideas:

- Something visual that you place in a spot you will see regularly.

- Develop a new habit, setting a reminder on your phone or putting a note in your diary to remind you to do it.

- Ask somebody that you trust to keep you accountable.

- Read a book or listen to talks online that will help you to explore your 'one thing' further.

Journeying Deeper into a Whole Life of Worship

Read *Whole Life Worship*

Creative, liberating, and inspiring, this book not only makes a passionate case for worship services that engage with people's Monday to Saturday lives but offers the biblical foundations, practical frameworks and a wealth of examples to fire the imagination of church and worship leaders whatever their stream or tradition. This book represents a significant contribution to establishing a sustainable culture of whole life discipleship in your church community.

'Packed with thoughtful provocation and practical innovation, this is a vital book for all those who lead in our churches.'

Krish Kandiah, Founder and Director, Home for Good

'Sam and Sara offer an important corrective to twenty-first-century church worship... the message is revolutionary if we will only take it on board.'

Mike Pilavachi, Soul Survivor

Visit: licc.org.uk/wholelifeworship

Sam & Sara Hargreaves

Whole Life WORSHIP

Empowering disciples for the frontline

Study *The Whole of Life for Christ*

Suppose for a moment that Jesus really is interested in every aspect of your life. This isn't just a nice idea we've come up with on our own, a comforting thought to make our daily lives seem more meaningful. It's threaded right through the Bible. The deeper we dig into God's word the more we're affirmed in our calling to be disciples of Jesus in every area of our lives. Whole-life gospel, wisdom, purpose, fruitfulness, mission, hope and worship – these seven studies developed by Antony Billington and Mark Greene in partnership with Keswick Ministries, work for both individuals and groups. We've also included material for leaders at the back of the book to help inform and prompt group discussion.

Visit: licc.org.uk/shop

Study *Fruitfulness on the Frontline*

Whether you're a student or retired, at the gym or at work, at the school gate or in the supermarket, these eight DVD-based sessions will help you and your group see how you can make a difference on your frontlines and support one another along the way. Combining biblical teaching from Mark Greene and inspiring real-life stories, the sessions explore 6Ms – six expressions of fruitfulness, that will open up a host of possibilities for you among the people you naturally meet, in the places you find yourself day by day.

Visit: licc.org.uk/fruitfulness

Explore *Whole Life Whole Bible*

Far from restricting our faith to the 'personal' sphere, God's word calls us to take the Lord of life into the whole of life. Ideal to be used as a daily devotional guide, *Whole Life Whole Bible* takes you through the unfolding story of Scripture in 50 short readings, that demonstrate how our lives are to be shaped by God's plan to restore a broken universe. The journey is sure to develop your thinking and fuel your imagination as you seek to live worshipfully in the light of God's word, whoever and wherever you are.

Visit: licc.org.uk/shop

Host a Whole Life Worship Day

In partnership with LICC, engageworship are offering a training day for church, worship and lay leaders to explore further the implications of whole life worship. Filled with worship and practical examples, the day begins by exploring the themes covered in the book, before offering a choice of two workshops: one focussed on service leading, the other on songs. The day is led by Sam & Sara Hargreaves and their band of experienced musicians.

If your church would be interested in hosting a Whole Life Worship Day, please email: **stefan.mcnally@licc.org.uk** for further information.

Visit the LICC Website

Whether you're looking to grow in your understanding of the Bible and its implications for your daily life, understand how to respond to the pressures and opportunities in today's world or workplace, or looking for resources to help as you lead a whole life disciple-making community, LICC's website is packed full of articles, videos, stories and content to help you on your journey.

Check it out at licc.org.uk